FROM THE POSSIBILITARIAN ARSENAL OF BELLIGERENT AND NOT SO BELLIGERENT SLOGANS

PETER SCHUMANN

FOMITE PRESS

Copyright © 2018   by Peter Schumann
All rights reserved. No part of this book may be reproduced
in any form or by any means without the prior written
consent, except in the case of brief quotations used in
reviews and certain other noncommercial uses permitted by
copyright law.

ISBN-13: 978-1-944388-69-0
Library of Congress Control Number: 2018958088
Fomite
58 Peru Street
Burlington, VT 05401

THIS IS THE BEGINNING OF THE POSSIBILITARIAN TAKEOVER OF SOCIETY. WE HEREWITH DISPOSE OF THE INCOMPETENT RULING CLASS BY UNDERTHROWING IT FROM THE TOES UP & IMMEDIATELY IMPLEMENTING THE 1000 ALTERNATIVES TO THE DESTRUCTIVE HABITS OF CAPITALISM. POLITICS MUST ABANDON ITS TRADITIONAL WAR & WEAPONS PREOCCUPATIONS & MAKE THE SEVERE HEALTH ISSUES OF OUR ONE AND ONLY MOTHER EARTH AND HER EARTHLINGS ITS PRIMARY CONCERN

FROM THE POSSIBILITARIAN ARSENAL OF BELLIGERENT SLOGANS

FROM THE POSSIBILITARIAN ARSENAL

MAN & HORIZON

HE WHO LULLS AWAY HIS LIFE SPAN IS STILL A STUDENT OF HIS SPAN OF LIFE

(1)

ESSENTIAL THIS

SPIRIT CONVINCES
IDEA PERSUADES
TRUTH SHATTERS

(2)

TOP WOMAN

THE DAY ITSELF IS SUSPECT OF COLLABORATION WITH ITS FRUSTRATED ATTEMPTS AT SUCCESS

WINDOW SPECTACLE

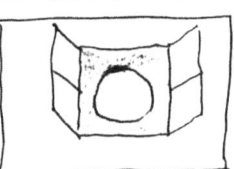

NIGHT ISN'T WHAT IT SEEMS TO BE. IT DOESN'T DIGNIFY OUR DISTURBANCES WITH DARKNESSES' PRE-ORDAINED PEACE

WIDE OPEN EXISTENCE

THE DAY'S FRENZY CULMINATES IN THE DAY'S LETHARGY WHICH IS NOT ACQUAINTED WITH SATISFACTION

DOWNHILL TRUTH

SITTING CONTRADICTS CREATION EVEN WHEN IT YIELDS CREATION

EPHEMERAL ENDLESSNESS

DANCING IS ONLY A SMALL PART OF THE NONSENSE WITH WHICH SENSE HAS TO BE INOCULATED

DERELATIONSHIP

RIOTOUS QUANTITIES PERFORM THEIR OPPOSITION TO QUANTITY

OVERWORKED SLEEP

THE DIFFICULTIES MUST BE DENIED THEIR IMPORTANCE BY APPROPRIATE UPHILL STRIDES

MAGNIFICENT TRASH

WELL TENDED GARDENS OF TOSSED-OFF TINCANS & BOTTLES INVENT PROGRESSIVE INGREDIENTS

OVERHEAD JOKE

HERE ←

OUR THOUGHTS ARE INHERITED & OUR EDUCATION OBLIGES US TO THEM. OUR OWN THOUGHTS HAVE NOT STARTED YET

(11)

PISSING ON THE DARK

THE DISTURBANCES OF THE POLITICAL PARTIES ARE COMEDIES THAT LAUGH AWAY THEIR TRAGIC INSIDES

(12)

FEET HAVE NOT
CLIMBED YET

FISTS HAVE
NOT POUNDED YET
BUT THE HORIZON'S DOOR
HAS CRACKED OPEN,
& THE POSSIBLE LIGHT
POURS THROUGH IT

#7

BREAD & PUPPET

THE NOT SO BELLIGERENT SLOGANS, FROM THE POSSIBILITARIAN ARSENAL

No 2

FROM THE POSSIBILITARIAN ARSENAL

FREEDOM ESCAPEES

NEGLIGENT MASSES VICTIMS OF STATE'S THOUGHTFULNESS

①

ANTI-EMPIRE BICYCLE

YOU, EXACT FRAGMENT OF TOTALITY, JOIN THE OTHER FRAGMENTS

②

KASPER

ILLOGICAL LUCK DEFEATS PRE-ORDAINED MISERY

③

SYSTEMATIC

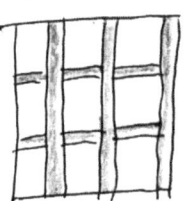

DETAINED AGENT DEALS WITH DETAINEES WHO ARE IMMUNE TO AGENTS UNLESS THEY ARE ALSO DETAINED

④

ROARING

UNLESS OUR FATHERS ARE RIGHT, WE MUST ABANDON WHAT'S CALLED LIFE & TRY SOMETHING BETTER

⑤

EXCELLENT TEARS

THE MANY BOW TO THE FEW BECAUSE THE FEW'S TRINKETS ARE MANY & ARE INTIMATELY TIED TO THE TRINKET PROFIT PARADISE

⑥

OLD HAT

FIXING THE ENGINE MEANS NOW YOU HAVE TO GO WHERE THE ENGINE WANTS YOU TO GO

AGAIN & AGAIN

THE BRIGHTEST LIGHT EVER HAPPENS SURPRISINGLY AUTOMATICALLY IN ORDER TO CONVINCE YOU OF LIGHT AGAIN & AGAIN

THE RAVENS HARMONY

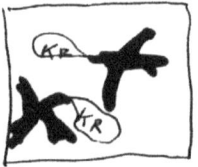

WE, IN HOT PURSUIT OF LIFE COMMITTED TO DEATH

OVERNESS

WE MINIATURE CITIZENS OF GRANDIOSE IDEALS SUFFER FROM THEIR MINIATURE IMPLEMENTATION

MY MITTENS' DAWN

THUMB & BRAIN
HITCHHIKE TO THE
NORTHEAST KINGDOM

IRRESPONSIBLE CLOCK

STRANGULATION BY TIME
AS BELLS DESIGNATE
TERMINATION OF LIFE'S
DETAILS

THE MEANING OF THE MOON & THE STARS IS

STOP THE BULLSHIT! STOP THE OIL! STOP THE WARS!

#9

BUTTERFLY HOVERING OVER SICKNESS

THE SPIRIT WON'T DO. YOU NEED THE MUSCLE TO JUMPSTART THE SPIRIT

WINGED MELANCHOLY

EXTRALONG EXTRACTION OF UNADMITTED SECRETS FERTILIZES BAD CONSCIENCE & CONSCIENCE

ELECTRICITY

THE FUN OF THE YOU ISN'T SEXUALITY. SEXUALITY IS GENERIC, THE YOU SPECIFIC

③

YOU TOO

THE WORK'S LEISURE AMUSES THE PRODUCT & THE WORKER

④

BRIDGING

WE ARE CONSTANTLY STIRRED UP & STIRRED DOWN BY WINDS THAT ORIGINATE IN AN UNFAMILIAR VOCABULARY

⑤

BEWARE: STAYING MUSCLES AT WORK

CAREFULLY TENDED CATASTROPHES RICHLY ORCHESTRATED LIKE SYMPHONIES ACHIEVE THEIR PEAK IN A BRILLIANT PRESTO SHORTLY BEFORE THE FINALE

⑥

OUR VERY OWN
PRIVATE DISTANCE

NOMADS NO MORE WE
TRAVEL BEYOND NOMAD'S REACH
DUTIFULLY SEDENTARILY

LABORING

FULLY UNAWARE OF THEIR
TRAGIC CIVILIZATION CIVILIANS
MUST CONTINUE TO ORDER
ITS LAVISH DESSERTS

UNDIRECTED
WHATFORWARD

HOLLERING TREES
INSTILL SILENCE IN
HUMANS

HALF A SNOW

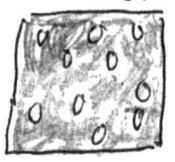

THE GOD SNOW
SUCCUMBS TO THE
LANDSCAPE GOD

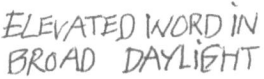

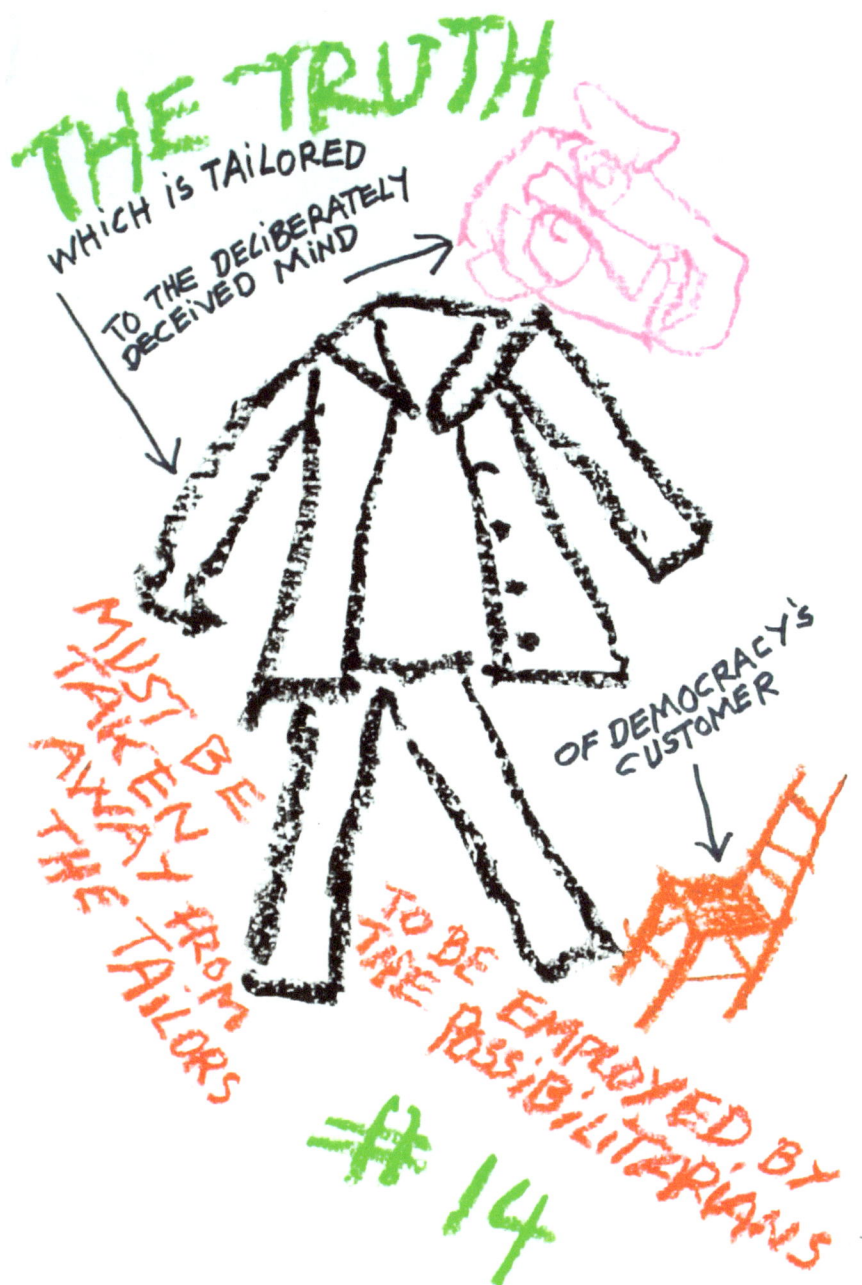

THE TRUTH WHICH IS MEASURED EXACTLY TO THE SIZE OF ITS CONSUMER MUST BE REMEASURED WITH THE POSSIBILITARIAN YARDSTICK

#14A

THE WHO STINKS
THE WHY OBSCURES POLITICS
THE WHERE TREMBLES FROM FEAR

ONLY THE WHAT IS CLEAR: WE NEED OUR ONE & ONLY POSSIBILITARIAN LIFE!

#15

NO WAY

THE PERFECT GOING IS THE AIMLESS ANYWHERE THAT DOES NOT KNOW WHERE IT ENDS UP

(1)

WHOLESALE-RETAIL

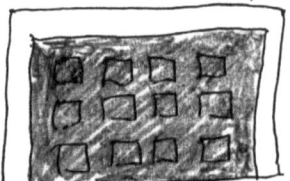

THE ISSUES BEYOND LIFE-PRETTYFICATION ARE AS MONSTROUS AS CAPITALISM ITSELF & OUR INCOMPETENT LANGUAGE MUST TACKLE THEM

(2)

OPPOSITE

NONE OF US ARE EXEMPT FROM SOLIDARITY WITH THE PRODUCTS OF THE EXACT OPPOSITE OF WHAT'S RIGHT

MORE

THE PRECISION ARBITRARINESS OF THE FUTURE IS THE MAGNET THAT PULLS THE ROOTS OUT OF THE PAST & MAKES THE PRESENT RACE TOWARDS THE UNKNOWN

SOUL'S SMOKE

SMOKE THAT STIMULATES PRETTY-FACED ILLUSION MOTIVATES WORK FORCE & WORKFORCE TO DONATE THEIR SOUL TO THE QUESTIONABLE ECONOMY

HEAD OVER HEELS

THE BUZZING FLY OF THE UNIVERSE INSOLENTLY OCCUPIES THE BEAUTIFUL AIR WITH ITS UNREHEARSED SONG

KRRR

REVILED FINISHLINE EYED WITH SUSPICION — WHIPPED ACROSS IT — INTO THE ARMS OF JUBILANT NORMALCY

⑦

ONWARD

INDECENT ASCEND INTO FORMALLY DRESSED SKY

⑧

OVER & BEYOND

RUSTING WAITERS & WAITRESSES SERVE THEIR STAINLESS STEEL CUSTOMERS FOR TIPS THAT ALLOW THEM TO CLEAN OFF THE RUST

⑨

WHATFORWARD

AS THE FORWARD COLLAPSES UNDER THE WEIGHT OF ITS OWN LOGIC, BEAUTIFUL NAKED REALITY TAKES OVER

⑩

ELOQUENT NOTHING

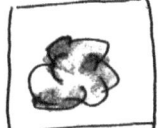

SICK CLOUDS HEALED BY CELEBRATORY SKY

 11

OVERSIZED DWARVES

THE NEVERGIANTS DETOUR THE COUNTRY'S GIANT HIGHWAY SYSTEM TIL ALL TRAFFIC IS FORCED TO SAIL INTO THE NEVER

 12

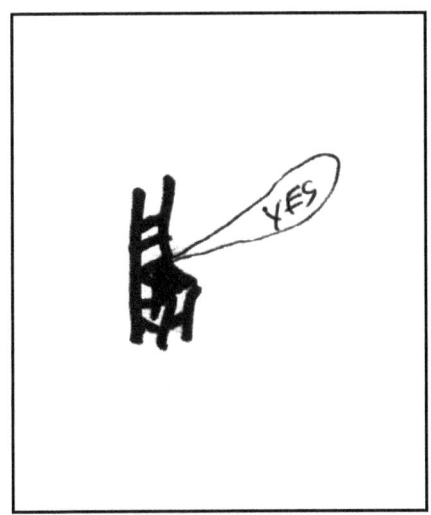

BY·POSSIBILITARIANS #16

THE IRRATIONALITY OF COMBAT ZONES IS DEMONSTRATED BY THE VEGETATION

THAT SPROUTS FROM THE CRACKS IN THE CEMENT #17

POSSIBILITARIAN BOMBS DON'T EXIST

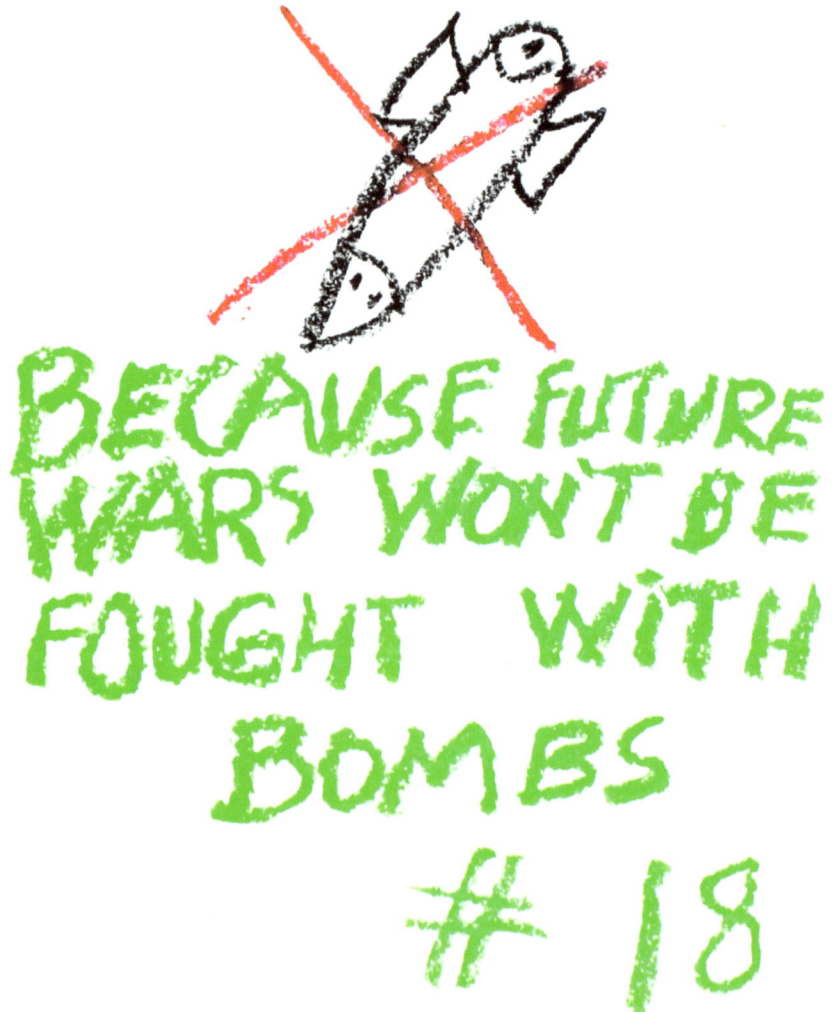

BECAUSE FUTURE WARS WON'T BE FOUGHT WITH BOMBS #18

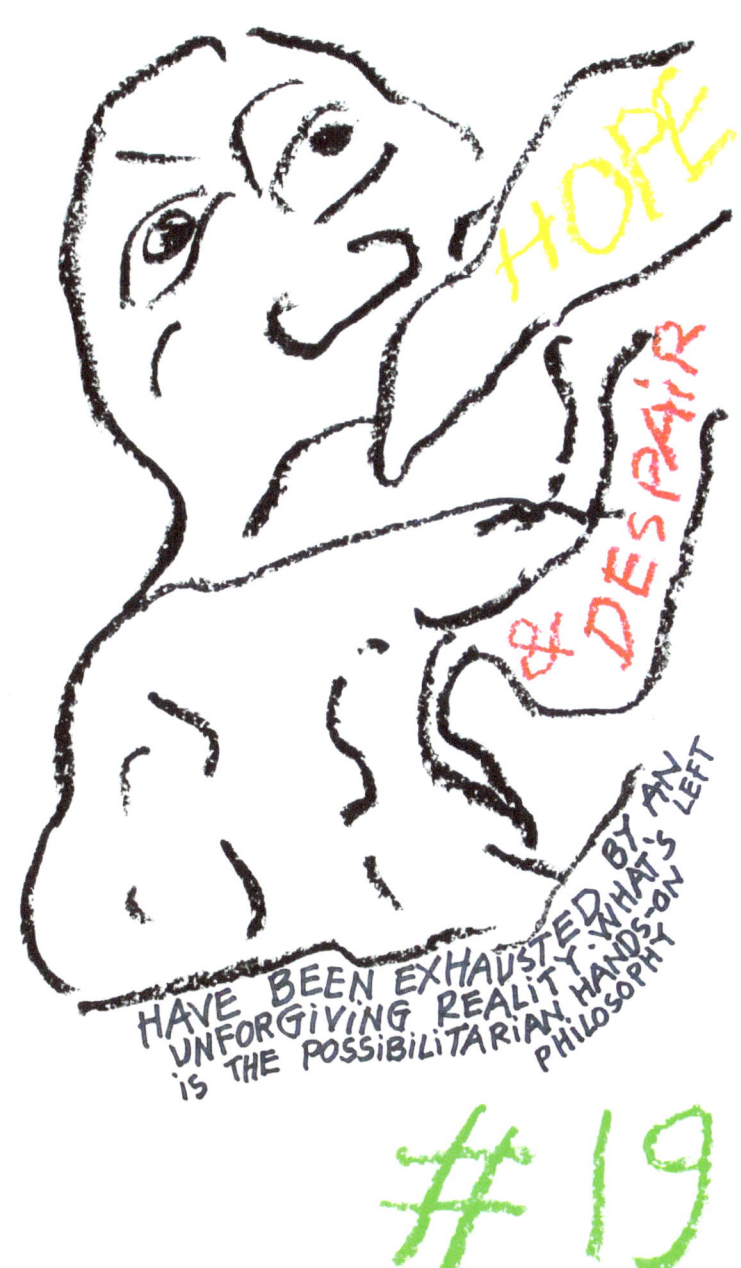

TO BE

WE WHO ARE NOT HERE YET - BUT HAVE ATTEMPTED IT A FEW TIMES - ARE LOOSELY KNIT NONENTITIES IN A UNIVERSE THAT IS NOT OURS

WE EXQUISITE IDIOTS OF NO SENSE MAKING IN THE REPUBLIC OF SENSE

UNTOUCHED TRUTH

WINTERSUN'S RAYS POURED FROM THE HADES ABOVE OVER THE DECREPIT PARADISE BELOW

③

PROFESSIONALISM

PROFESSIONAL BRUTALITY EMPLOYED FOR HUMANITARIAN PURPOSES. SUPREMACIST MALE IN SCOPE; NOT A DISEASE BUT A LEGITIMATE HUMAN STRENGTH, CONTINUES TO RETARD THE RACE

④

INDISTINCTION

DISTINCT FURY TARGETS THE INDISTINCT ABUNDANCE THAT PROUDLY DISGUISES DEATH & DESTRUCTION

⑤

DETRITUS GLORIOSOS

LUST'S FATHER, THE ANONYMOUS ON HIS THRONE, NEWLY DETHRONED BY BRAND NEW ECONOMICALLY CORRECT LUSTS

⑥

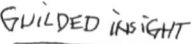
GUILDED INSIGHT

THE ROOM'S WEALTH, THE ACCUMULATED GLORY OF BOOKSHELVES & PAGES, SHRINKS TO A PINSIZE FRAGMENT OF A QUESTIONMARK:
    WHAT NEXT?

 7

FAT

DE-EMPHASIZING THE IMPORTANCES WHICH ARE FAT & UNYIELDING & SUPPLYING THEM WITH A PROLETARIAN DIET

⑧

ALLOWING

DERAILED OVERREALITY SPREAD INTO TODAY'S MUD MUST ALLOW

    REALITY

  TO EMERGE
FROM THE WRECKAGE

 9

Nº 1

SINISTER ASSESSMENT OF DEMOCRACY'S CONSISTENT SLAVERIES MUST ASSIST THEIR DESTRUCTION

 10

MATERIAL

WE CONTAINERS FULL OF RADIO & OTHER VERBAGES ARE ALSO REGULARILY EMPTY AS THE DUMPTRUCK CLEANS US OUT TO RECEIVE NEW GARBAGE

(11)

EX VOTO

LAME SOUL'S SPRINT TO JOYOUS FINISHLINE

(12)

HELLFIRE EXHUBERANCE
INHERITED FROM
LACERATED BONES &
BEINGS

RE-EMPLOYED
FOR POSSIBILITARIAN
PURPOSES

21

MUST

THINKING WHICH CANNOT ALTER AUTHORITY, SPEECH WHICH CANNOT CHANGE WAR, HABIT WHICH CANNOT DEFEAT BRUTALITY ALL MUST REVOLUTIONIZE

①

BY THE LIGHT OF THE DAY

LIFE'S LOVE IS A CONDENSED QUANTITY, AN EXACT MINIMUM, COMPOSED OF THE ENDEFFECTS OF THE TOO MUCH

②

ABOVE ALL

BRUTALITY'S CLAIM OF SIMPLE SOLUTION KEEPS ITS ORGANIZATION ABOVE ALL GOVERNMENT INSTRUMENTS & GUARANTEES THE FINAL SOLUTION

OPPOSITION

ONLY WE THE ONLIES CAN MUSTER THE COURAGE TO OPPOSE OUR ONLYNESS

DIVINE CRY

THE ANTIQUE OUTCRY OF THE BEASTLY SELF AROUSES THE BEAUTY WHICH IS THE BEAST

EACH OTHER

THAT WHICH LOVES EACH OTHER IS FROM THE WIND OF IMPERMANENCE & SETTLES THE SOUL INTO STONE PERMANENCE

PRIVILEGE

THE PRIVILEGED STATUS OF 1-FOOT IN THE GRAVE SENIORS WITH THEIR 100 PERMISSIONS TO LET GO & NOT PURSUE IS BASED ON THEIR DOWN-SIZED PHILOSOPHY OF RELEVANCES & MEANINGS

WHERE

IMAGINATION'S AUTHORITY, ANONYMOUS COPY OF THE FLESH SELF, IS PUT IN CHARGE WHERE ALL IMAGINATION FAILS

HAIRCUT & ECSTASY

WE TRIM OUR BEARDS TO LIGHTEN OUR SUBSTANCE & FALL DOWN THE STAIRS TO BREAK OUR HAIRDO IN HALF & FINALLY GET OLD TO RECAPTURE THE ORIGINAL ECSTASY

TOOTHPASTE

THE GRIN OF UNHAPPINESS PRETENDING TO BE OTHERWISE, SYMBOL OF TOOTHPASTE & PERFECT STATE OF AFFAIRS AS IN FAMILY'S PERFECTION, INCLUDES VIOLENT TRUE LOVE

NOT YET

OUR WOODPILE DWINDLES LIKE OUR WINTER SOUL

11

INTENSITY

PAIN DEMONS, RETARDERS OF HEALTH, ELEVATORS OF INVISIBLE DETAILS ENHANCE LIFE'S MINIMALISM

12

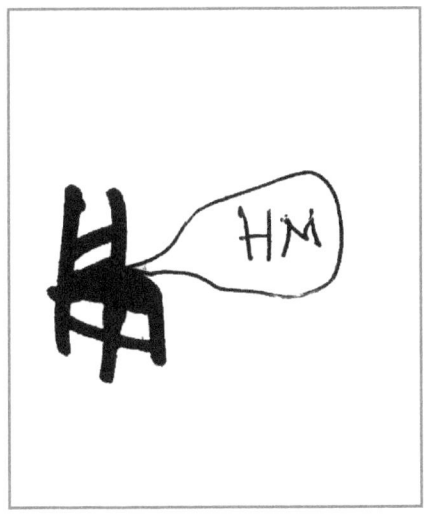

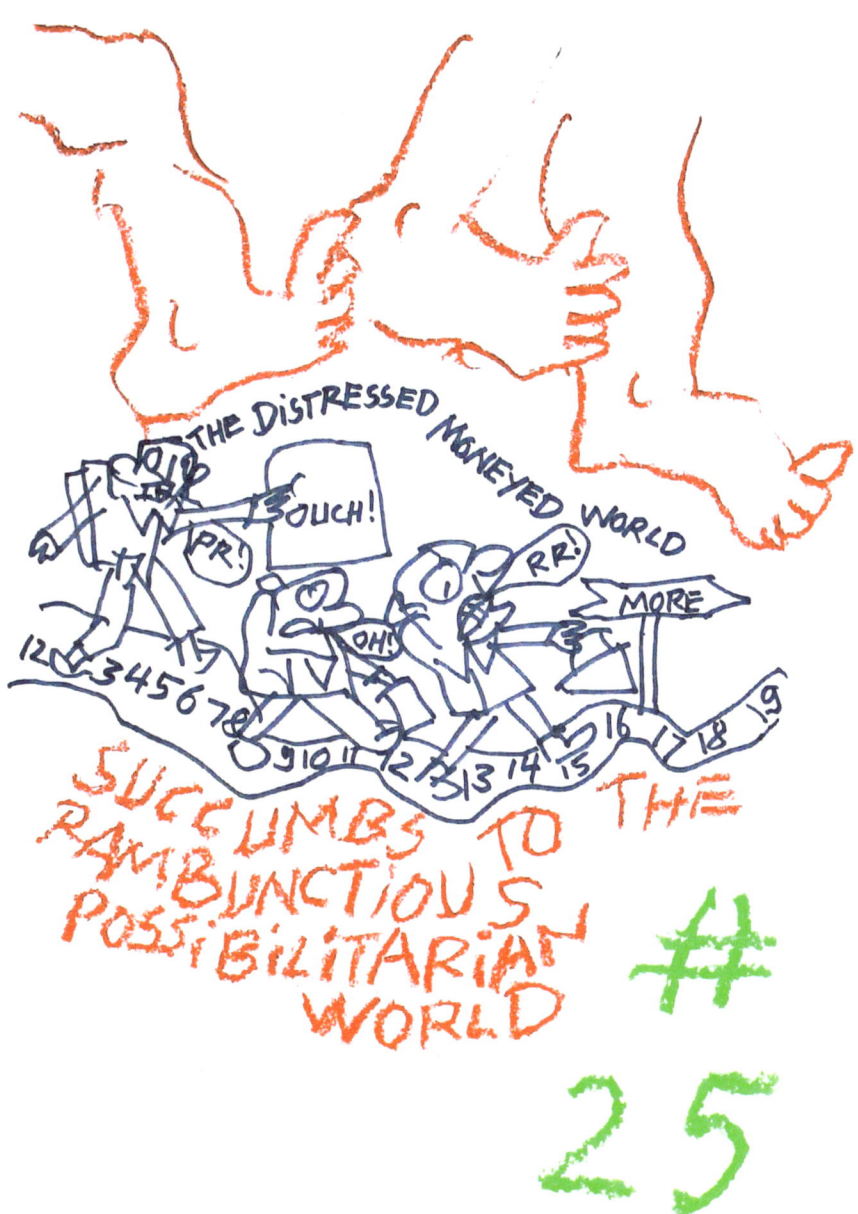

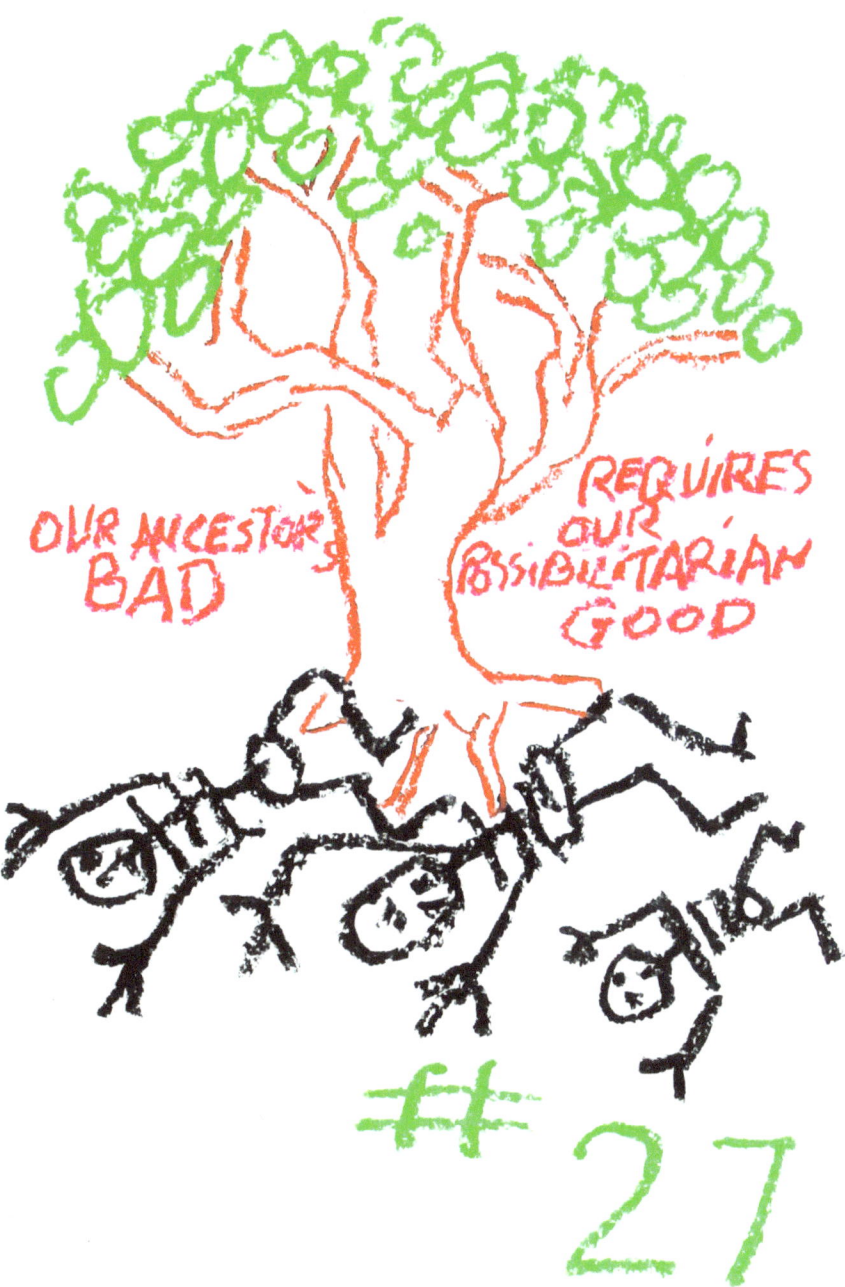

LA-LA-LA

ARCHITECTURE OF ICYCLES SUPPORTING THE WINTER AIR THAT CLAIMS OWNERSHIP OF THE HOUSE

①

COUGHING

SICK LITTLENESS WANDERING LEISURELY OVER BLOSSOMING SNOW MEADOW CURES ITS COUGH IN TERMINALLY SICK PINE FOREST TENDED BY RAVENS

②

M.A.D.

TOTALITARIAN CONVICTION STRAIGHT FROM THE PREACHER'S PULPIT EMPOWERS FAKE LOVE TO COMMIT REAL WAR

WORLD

SENSING THE PREDICTABLE NONSENSE OF WHAT'S AHEAD YOU NEED TO CHECK YOUR SENSIBILITIES

OUR WE

ARSEKICKING UPWARD DETERIORATES REGULARLY IN OUR POLITICAL ECONOMY WHICH GLORIFIES ARSEKICKING

JOURNEY

COMING GENTLY TO THE OVERCOMING THAT THE HEAD NEEDS WHEN IT CONSIDERS TRAVELLING TO ITS OBLIGATIONS

THE

RARE MINIMAL ENGAGEMENT OF SCREAMING UNDONES

⑦

SILENCE

VOLUNTARY NOT DOING IN RESPONSE TO PERFECTIONIST OVERLOAD PRODUCES THE PAUSES THAT MUSIC ASKS FOR

⑧

AFTER COFFEE

SEE EAT GO OVER THERE GO EAT SEE OVER THEN AFTER OVER THERE GO EAT AFTER THINK AFTER COFFEE

⑨

OUR

WE WITH THE NOTHING AT OUR DISPOSAL ADDRESS THE EVERYTHING

⑩

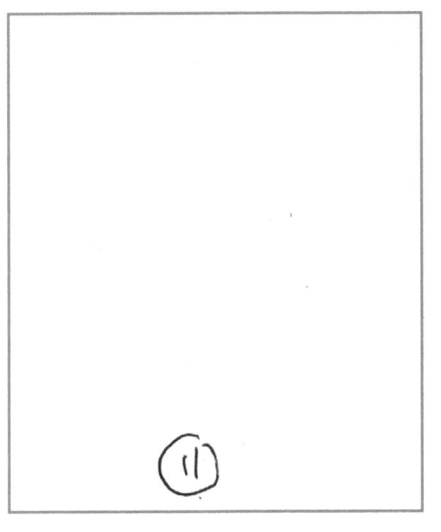

(11)

(12)

THE ECONOMY'S FASCISM

MUST BE DEFEATED BY THE POSSIBILITARIAN UNDERCLASS

\#30

BOOK DESIGN & EDIT BY
DONNA BISTER & MARC ESTRIN

THE TERM POSSIBILITARIAN IS FROM MARC ESTRIN'S NOVEL INSECT DREAMS REFERRING TO THE MOGLISCHKEITSMENSCH IN ROBERT MUSIL'S NOVEL DER MANN OHNE EIGENSCHAFTEN & WAS WIDELY USED IN BREAD & PUPPET PRODUCTIONS EVER SINCE.

www.ingramcontent.com/pod-product-compliance
Lightning Source LLC
Chambersburg PA
CBHW040201100526
44591CB00006B/58